CANADA

SALLY GARRINGTON

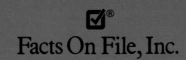

Facts On File, Inc.

TITLES IN THE COUNTRIES OF THE WORLD SERIES:

ARGENTINA • AUSTRALIA • BRAZIL • CANADA • CHINA
EGYPT • FRANCE • GERMANY • INDIA • ITALY • JAPAN
KENYA • MEXICO • NIGERIA • POLAND • UNITED KINGDOM
UNITED STATES • VIETNAM

Canada

Facts On File, Inc.
132 West 31st Street
New York NY 10001

Library of Congress Cataloging-in-Publication Data

Garrington, Sally
   Canada / Sally Garrington
      p. cm. — (Countries of the world)
   Includes index.
   ISBN 0-8160-6009-6
   1. Canada—Juvenile literature. I. Title. II. Countries of the world (Facts On File, Inc.)
F1008.2.G37 2005
971—dc22   2005040676

Facts On File books are available at special discounts when purchased in bulk quantities for businesses, associations, institutions, or sales promotions. Please call our Special Sales Department in New York at (212) 967-8800 or (800) 322-8755.

You can find Facts On File on the World Wide Web at
http://www.factsonfile.com.

Printed in China by Leo Paper Products Ltd.

10 9 8 7 6 5 4 3 2 1

Endpapers (front): A spectacular view of the Toronto skyline at night.
Title page: Three Inuit children playing on ice floes in Village Harbor, Nunavut.
Imprint and Contents pages: Snowboarders appreciating Vancouver's dramatic landscape.
Endpapers (back): A stunning view of Gwaii Haanas National Park, British Columbia.

Editor: Daniel Rogers
Designer: Victoria Webb
Picture researchers: Lynda Lines and Frances Bailey
Map artwork: Peter Bull
Charts and graphs: Encompass Graphics, Ltd.

Photograph acknowledgments:
front cover top (Bill Bachman/Image Works, Topham Picturepoint); front cover upper middle (Blue Shadows, Alamy); front cover lower middle, 12 top, 20, 47 (Gunter Mark Photography, Corbis); front cover bottom, front and back endpapers, 6–7, 24 bottom, 32, 46, 53, 61 (Canadian High Commission); 5 (Momatuik Eastcott/Image Works, Topham Picturepoint); 9 (Kike Kalvo, Ecoscene); 10, 57 bottom (Matthew Bolton, Ecoscene); 11 (Guy Menendez, Ecoscene); 12 bottom (Rich Kirchner, NHPA); 13, 35 (Larry MacDougall, Still Pictures); 14 top (Fotoware, Topham Picturepoint); 14 bottom (SIPA, Rex Features); 16 (Paul A. Souders, Corbis); 17 top (Lowell Georgia, Corbis); 17 bottom (Photri, Topham Picturepoint); 18 (Joseph Sohm/Image Works, Topham Picturepoint); 19, 22 top (Dorothy Littell Greco/Image Works, Topham Picturepoint); 22 bottom (Pier 21 Society); 23, 25, 31 (Mark Henley); 24 top (Paul Thompson, Eye Ubiquitous); 26 bottom (B & C Alexander, Still Pictures); 27 top (Image Works, Topham Picturepoint); 27 bottom, 47 top (B & C Alexander, Alamy); 29 top, 42 top (TS/Keystone USA, Rex Features); 29 bottom (Norm Betts, Rex Features); 30, 36 (Will Waldron/Image Works, Topham Picturepoint); 33 top (Bob Battersby, Eye Ubiquitous); 33 bottom (Eye Ubiquitous); 34, 44 (Shaun Best, Reuters); 37 (Blue Shadows, Alamy); 38, 50 (Hans-Jurgen Burkard, Network Photographers); 39 (Frank Grant, ImageState); 40 (Sean O'Neill, Alamy); 41 (Pierre Dunnigan, Still Pictures); 42 bottom (Andy Clark, Reuters); 45 (Jim Young, Reuters); 48 (Jochen Tack, Still Pictures); 49 (William A. Blake, Corbis); 51 top (Graham Kitching, Ecoscene); 51 bottom (Karen Tweedy-Holmes, Corbis); 52, 60 (Corbis Digital Stock); 54 (PA, Topham Picturepoint); 55 (Eriko Sugita); 56 (Martin Bond, Still Pictures); 57 top (Alan Watson, Still Pictures).

First published by Evans Brothers Limited, 2A Portman Mansions, Chiltern Street, London W1U 6NR, United Kingdom.

This edition published under license from Evans Brothers Limited. All rights reserved.

CONTENTS

The Canadian flag features a maple leaf, the country's symbol, and two red bars on a white background. Red and white are the national colors of Canada.

INTRODUCING CANADA

An aerial view of the port city of Vancouver, British Columbia.

Canada is the second-largest country in the world after Russia, and is somewhat larger than the United States. It spreads across six time zones and it is bordered on three sides by oceans: the Arctic to the north, the Pacific to the west and the Atlantic to the east. Its only land borders, to the south and west, are with the United States. It is farther to travel from Halifax in the east of Canada to Whitehorse in the west than from London in the United Kingdom to Halifax, Canada.

CONTRASTING LANDSCAPES

Landscapes vary from the vast snow- and ice-covered areas of the far north to the flat and seemingly endless plains of the center, and from the rugged coasts of Nova Scotia to the high mountains of the west. Isolation resulting from huge distances, harsh climates and a sometimes-difficult terrain meant that Canada's settlement developed initially in small pockets.

PROVINCES AND TERRITORIES OF CANADA

ARCTIC OCEAN

ALASKA (USA)

YUKON TERRITORY

NORTHWEST TERRITORIES

NUNAVUT

N

Whitehorse

Yellowknife

Baker Lake

Iqaluit

BRITISH COLUMBIA

Kitimat

ALBERTA

Edmonton

Churchill

Hudson Bay

NEWFOUNDLAND AND LABRADOR

Grates Cove

St John's

MANITOBA

Calgary

SASKATCHEWAN

QUEBEC

PRINCE EDWARD ISLAND

Vancouver Island

Whistler

Victoria

Vancouver

Kimberley

Regina

Winnipeg

ONTARIO

NEW BRUNSWICK

Charlottetown

NOVA SCOTIA

Quebec

St John

Halifax

Montreal

PACIFIC OCEAN

UNITED STATES OF AMERICA

Kanata

Ottawa

Toronto

ATLANTIC OCEAN

0   1500 km
0   1000 miles

A caribou (or reindeer) in a tundra landscape in northern Manitoba.

A DIVERSE PEOPLE

The name Canada comes from a Huron-Iroquois word – *kanata* – meaning village or settlement. Native Americans, who are known in Canada as First Nation peoples, form only a small percentage of today's multicultural population. Large numbers (60 percent) of Canadians are descended from English, Welsh, Irish and Scottish immigrants but nearly a quarter of the country is French speaking and of French descent. These two main groupings represent the origins of modern Canada, in that it was the French followed by the English who first explored and settled Canada. The country still has large numbers of immigrants. Most now come from Asian countries although there is a continuing, but much smaller, flow from Europe.

Large areas of the country are sparsely populated, with 90 percent of Canadians living on just 12 percent of the land area. In fact, 80 percent of the population lives within 160km of the US border.

RICH RESOURCES

Canada is rich in natural resources, such as timber, furs and fish, and it also has important mineral reserves. A large proportion of Canada's trade and industries still relies on semifinished raw materials, which is unusual for a developed nation. Its main exports include timber and timber products, energy, and foodstuffs, and it imports manufactured goods. This pattern is changing now that Canada has become a world leader in high-tech industries, especially biotechnology.

THE COUNTRY OF CANADA

Canada became a country in 1867, although some of today's provinces were not included. The last province to join the Dominion of Canada was Newfoundland, in 1949. Today Canada consists of 10 provinces and three territories. The newest territory is Nunavut, which was created in 1999 and is a largely self-governing area. The provinces have a lot of individual power and are responsible for education, health and other services. The territories are funded and controlled by the national government in Ottawa. Although Canada has a prime minister and is a parliamentary democracy, its head of state is still the English monarch, Queen Elizabeth II. Some French-speaking Canadians find this hard to accept.

Canada has one of the highest standards of living in the world, and together with an exceptionally high quality of life, this has meant that it continues to attract immigrants.

KEY DATA

Official Name:	Canada
Area:	9,971,000km^2
Highest Point:	Mount Logan 5,959m
Population:	31,752,842 (2004 est.)
Capital City:	Ottawa (pop. 1,128,900)

Main Cities:
  Toronto (pop. 5,029,900)
  Montreal (pop. 3,548,800)
  Vancouver (pop. 2,122,700)

GDP Per Capita:	US$29,480*
Currency:	Canadian dollar (Can$)
Exchange Rate:	US$1 = Can$1.22 £1 = Can$2.29

*(2002) Calculated on Purchasing Power Parity basis
Sources: *CIA World Factbook, 2004*; World Bank; UN Human Development Report, 2004

LANDSCAPE AND CLIMATE

Warmth and lots of rainfall enable temperate rain forest to grow in the southwest of British Columbia.

THE LANDSCAPES OF CANADA

The rocks that lie beneath Canada range from the ancient rocks that form the Canadian Shield to the much younger rocks that make up the mountains of the west. Overlying some areas are deposits left by the last ice age, which ended around 10,000 years ago.

THE WESTERN MOUNTAINS

In the west of Canada there are two parallel mountain chains that run in a north-to-south direction. Collectively known as the Western Cordillera, they consist of the Rockies (a continuation of the mountains of the same name in the United States) to the east and the Coast Range to the west. East to west they are 700km wide and dominate the landscapes of western Canada. The highest point in Canada, Mount Logan (5,959m), is part of the Coast Range. The mountains of the Western Cordillera are young fold mountains, and they are still growing about 2cm taller every year. This is due to the pressure the Pacific tectonic plate exerts as it is subducted beneath the North American plate, which can cause earthquakes and volcanic eruptions. Volcanoes such as Mount Meager are part of the same chain as Mount St Helens in the United States, which last erupted in 1980.

In the western mountains, vegetation changes with altitude (height above sea level). There are dense forests on the lower slopes, including some temperate rain forest in the southwest of the Coast Range. Higher up the mountains, this vegetation becomes alpine meadows where it is too cold for trees to grow. Eventually alpine meadows give way to alpine tundra, where only mosses, lichens and some hardy grasses are able to grow, succeeded by snowfields at the tops of the mountains.

ARCTIC
OCEAN

Arctic

Lowlands

Beaufort
Sea

*Baffin
Bay*

Baffin Island

Davis Strait

N

ALASKA
(USA)

Mackenzie River

▲ *Mt. Logan*

*Great Bear
Lake*

LABRADOR
SEA

*Great Slave
Lake*

Slave River

Peace River

*Lake
Athabasca*

Liard River

Churchill River

Nelson River

*Hudson

Bay*

La Grande River

Eagle River

*Columbia
Icefield*

*Great

Plains*

C a n a d i a n   *S h i e l d*

*James
Bay*

*Gaspé
Peninsula*

*Meager
Volcano* ▲

*Lake
Winnipeg*

St. Lawrence River

*Vancouver
Island*

PACIFIC

OCEAN

UNITED STATES OF AMERICA

Lake Superior

*Bay of
Fundy*

0   1500 km

0   1000 miles

*Lake
Huron*

Lake Michigan

*Lake
Ontario*

*Lake
Erie*

ATLANTIC

OCEAN

THE GREAT PLAINS

This generally flat area consists of three huge terraces, hundreds of kilometers across, which become lower toward the east. At the foot of the Rocky Mountains the Plains are 1,080m high but by their eastern edge in Manitoba they are only 200m above sea level.

The Plains have deep soils over much of their area, made up of deposits left by the last ice age. This glaciation also left lakes as the ice melted, creating particularly large ones, such as the Great Slave Lake, Great Bear Lake, Lake Athabasca and Lake Winnipeg along the junction with the older rocks of the Canadian Shield to the east. Coal, oil, gas and mineral deposits are found in the rocks that underlie the Plains.

In the southern plains it is too dry for trees to grow. Prairie grasses, growing in huge open expanses, are the natural vegetation of the area. Farther north, where the evaporation rates are lower, there are forests. At about 60° north latitude the forests change to tundra, where it is too cold for trees to grow.

The dry climate of the prairies allows only grasses and drought-resistant plants to thrive.

THE CANADIAN SHIELD

The Canadian Shield is a huge, bowl-shaped region with its center at Hudson Bay. It underlies more than half of the area of Canada and is made up of some of the oldest rocks in the world. The rocks are thought to be nearly 4 billion years old – almost as old as the Earth itself. They have been worn down over time to produce a generally low landscape, with mountains at the edges of the bowl. These ancient rocks contain a wealth of minerals. During the last ice age, ice sheets and glaciers scoured the surface of the shield. When they melted, the scoured material was washed away and deposited elsewhere, such as in the Great Plains. The rocks of the Canadian Shield are very hard, with thin soils overlying them, and the landscape is dotted with large numbers of lakes left over from the last ice age.

The vegetation of the shield is mainly coniferous forest, including spruce, larch and pine trees. Beyond 60° north latitude (the tree line) this changes to tundra vegetation and muskeg. Muskeg is the name for peat bog in North America, and these bogs cover large

ABOVE: A view of a muskeg (or peat bog) landscape in Yukon Territory.

BELOW: The long, thick coat of the musk ox helps it survive the freezing tundra winters.

areas of Canada. The main vegetation is sphagnum moss, which can hold up to 30 times its own weight of water. The moss prevents water from draining through the soil and creates a wet, acidic environment. Plants do not readily decompose in muskeg because no air can get to them, so within its layers are plants at different stages of decomposition.

The Arctic Lowlands lie to the northwest of the Canadian Shield. They are made up of more recent sedimentary rocks that in some places overlie the shield rocks. North of the shield, tundra vegetation takes over. Much of the area is underlain by permafrost – a layer of soil below the surface that remains permanently frozen. Mosses and lichens grow in the tundra as well as specialized grasses, such as cotton grass, that can cope with the cold and wet conditions. In the brief northern summer, the upper layers of soil thaw but the permafrost layer acts like impermeable rock, preventing water from draining away. The land becomes waterlogged, enabling it to support a range of flowers and grasses. It also becomes the breeding ground for huge swarms of biting insects, such as mosquitoes. Caribou and musk ox live in these areas, as well as small rodents and the birds of prey that feed on them.

LOWLANDS OF THE ST LAWRENCE AND THE GREAT LAKES

This area of Canada represents 3 percent of the country's total landmass. It is a bowl-shaped area with fertile soils left by the last ice age. The lowlands have more than half of Canada's best farmland and are an important agricultural area. The natural vegetation of the region is deciduous woodland, though much has been cleared for farming and development.

THE APPALACHIANS

The Appalachians are a continuation of the mountain range of the same name in the United States. In this area the once-high mountains have been reduced by erosion to create a landscape of rolling hills and narrow valleys. The region is about 600km wide and has a rocky coastline with many inlets.

As a result of the area's hard rock and its cool, wet climate, the soils are generally poor. Its highest points are on the Gaspé Peninsula in Quebec (1,200m). The natural vegetation is mixed woodland of coniferous and deciduous trees, and up to 66 percent of this remains.

The rocky coastline around the fishing village of Grates Cove is typical of Newfoundland.

People enjoying the summer sunshine in Toronto, Ontario.

CLIMATE
PACIFIC COASTLANDS

Between the Pacific Ocean and the Western Cordillera is a narrow belt where the climate is warm and damp. The mountains force rain-bearing winds to rise up over them, and as they rise, they drop their load of rain on the western slopes, creating very moist conditions. In the southwest, where it is warmest, this gives rise to conditions that can support temperate rain forest.

MOUNTAIN CLIMATE

In the mountain ranges the temperature is warm in the valleys and gets progressively colder as the height increases, up to the snowfields at the peaks where it is rarely above freezing. Much of the sunlight that reaches this area is reflected away by the bright snow before it can heat up the land. Wind speeds are much greater at the tops of mountains than in the valleys.

CONTINENTAL CLIMATE

Rainfall is low in Canada's Great Plains, especially in the west, because nearly all the rain has fallen on the other side of the mountain ranges; it is known as a rain-shadow area. Far from the moderating influence of the sea, this region experiences very harsh winters and summers that can be quite hot. In the summer, rapid heating can result in violent thunderstorms with hailstones so large that they can damage crops. The rapid heating can also give rise to tornadoes.

Drought can have a significant impact in this area. In 2001–2002, a severe drought affected 65 percent of the prairie crop-growing area and reduced crop production by 66 percent. This reduced the amount of wheat available for export and caused a

CASE STUDY
THE ICE STORM OF 1998

An ice storm occurs when supercooled rain falls, and as soon as it touches an object or the ground it freezes. Often, such storms are accompanied by strong winds and very low temperatures. In January 1998, a huge ice storm hit southern Ontario, Quebec, New Brunswick and Nova Scotia. Twenty-eight people died and 945 were injured. Thousands of electricity pylons buckled under the weight of ice and 10 percent of Canada's population was without electricity for at least a week.

One of the many electric pylons that buckled under the weight of the ice during the 1998 ice storm.

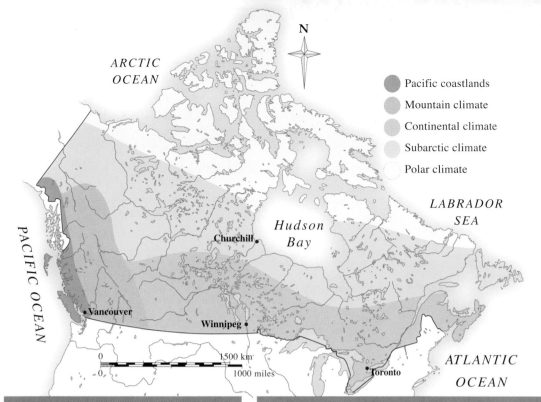

Pacific coastlands
Mountain climate
Continental climate
Subarctic climate
Polar climate

CLIMATE ZONES

loss of jobs that were dependent upon wheat production.

This is also the area that feels the effect of the Chinook – a warm wind that blows down the eastern side of the Rockies. It usually occurs in winter or spring and can cause an early thaw of the winter snows.

SUBARCTIC AND POLAR CLIMATES

Much of Canada is subject to long, cold, dark winters and brief summers, which are typical of high latitudes. The temperature is above freezing for only one to four months of the year, and even then only the upper layers of soil thaw. In the far north the sun barely rises above the horizon in winter, and in summer the sun never totally sets. This severe climate has limited the settlement of much of Canada, although people such as the Inuit (formerly known as the Eskimo) are well adapted to its harshness.

TEMPERATURE AND RAINFALL

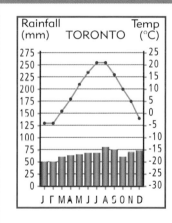

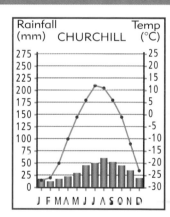

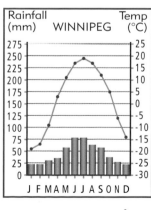

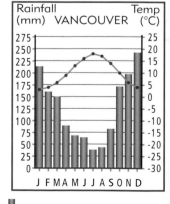

KEY:

 Temperature

 Rainfall

THE RIVERS OF CANADA

Canada has more rivers and lakes than any other country, and 7 percent of the world's fresh water flows through them. The rivers are used for recreation, as important transport links and as a water supply for settlements. Another important use of river flow in Canada is in the production of hydroelectric power (HEP).

RIVERS UNDER THREAT

Even in Canada, where much of the land is classified as wilderness, the rivers are under threat from a variety of sources. Rivers that flow through urban areas are exposed to industrial pollution and sewage effluent. Riverside habitats are also lost when they are built on as a result of town or city expansion.

CASE STUDY
THE FRASER RIVER

The Airtram carries visitors down to view the salmon fishways in the Fraser River Canyon, British Columbia.

The Fraser River is the largest river in British Columbia and drains an area the size of Great Britain (232,300km^2). It rises in the Rocky Mountains and flows for 1,370km until it empties into the Pacific Ocean near Vancouver. The valley of the Fraser River was used for the route of the Canadian Pacific Railway and, later, the Trans-Canada Highway, since it offered a way through the mountains. These developments opened up the west of Canada. The Fraser River Basin contains important areas of timber production, as well as sites for the production of HEP. This power is used in industries such as aluminum smelting. The basin generates 10 percent of the gross domestic product (GDP) of the whole of Canada.

The Fraser is the most important river in the world for salmon fishing. The fish are caught as they make their way upriver to spawn every year. Where the tributaries of the river have been dammed for HEP production, salmon numbers have greatly decreased, or the fish has become extinct in that stretch.

As the river drops toward the Pacific Ocean it forms a large, fertile floodplain, which is an important area for agriculture. Its delta provides an ideal breeding ground for wildfowl but special reserves have had to be created to protect birds from the continued growth of the city of Vancouver.

CASE STUDY
THE MACKENZIE RIVER – A VITAL COMMUNICATION LINK

The Mackenzie is Canada's longest river and drains a massive 1,805,200km² area. Including its tributaries, it runs for 4,241km and flows north into the Beaufort Sea via a large delta. Both the river and its delta are important areas for wildlife. There is oil drilling at Norman Wells but further exploitation of oil and gas is on hold for the time being as the First Nations decide what is best for the region as a whole.

The Mackenzie is an important communication route to isolated settlements along its course that cannot be reached by road. From June to October, supplies can be transported to these communities from Yellowknife on Great Slave Lake. They are carried upriver on barges, and then by sea to Inuit communities in the high Arctic.

RIGHT: An aerial view of the Mackenzie River delta, Northwest Territories.

LEFT: The muskrat is superbly adapted to the watery habitat of the Mackenzie delta.

Rivers in wilderness areas, far from centers of population, can also be under threat. The main threat is from the building of large-scale dams that alter a river's flow and its ecosystems. If a mining operation is carried out near a river, it can pollute the water and affect the aquatic life. However, Canada still has large numbers of wild rivers that have had little or no human activity affecting them.

THE GREAT LAKES AND THE ST LAWRENCE SEAWAY

A view of the Horseshoe Falls from the Canadian side, a barrier to river trade until the Welland Canal was built.

The five Great Lakes – Superior, Michigan, Huron, Erie and Ontario – are a legacy of the last ice age. The border between the United States and Canada runs through four of them, with only Lake Michigan being completely within the United States. The Great Lakes and the St Lawrence River combined make up the largest freshwater system on Earth.

THE GREAT LAKES

Lake Superior is the largest lake in the world. Thunder Bay on its shores is the third-largest freshwater port in Canada and it exports most of Canada's wheat from the west. Lake Huron is popular for outdoor pursuits, although it has some industrial towns, including Windsor, on its southern shores. Lake Erie is the shallowest of the lakes and is the only one that can completely freeze over. At its eastern outlet are the Niagara Falls which lead into Lake Ontario. The falls consist of the American and Bridal Veil Falls over the US border and the larger Horseshoe Falls on the Canadian side. It was impossible for large ships to pass beyond Niagara Falls until the present-day Welland Canal was completed in 1932. It runs parallel to the falls and allows ships to pass from Lake Erie into Lake Ontario via a system of eight locks. The lake closest to the Atlantic, Lake Ontario, has the smallest surface area

GREAT LAKES FACTS

	LENGTH km	MAX DEPTH m	TOTAL AREA km^2
Lake Superior	563	406	82,100
Lake Huron	332	229	59,600
Lake Erie	388	64	25,700
Lake Ontario	311	244	18,960
(Lake Michigan, USA)	(494)	(282)	(57,800)

and is the most polluted of the lakes, partly because it is the center of Canada's largest industrial and commercial areas. Also, water flows into Lake Ontario after passing through the other lakes, so it receives much of their pollution too.

The water levels in the Great Lakes are falling, and dredging has to be carried out daily in some parts of the lakes to allow the passage of ships. Global warming is blamed for an increased rate of evaporation, and recent droughts have reduced the flow of water into the Great Lakes system.

FROM THE LAKES TO THE SEA

The St Lawrence River is one of the shortest major rivers in the world, at 1,287km. It connects the Great Lakes to the Atlantic Ocean and so to markets in Europe and beyond. The St Lawrence Seaway, a series of canals, dams and locks opened in 1959, was jointly constructed by Canada and the United States to allow ships passage between the Great Lakes and the Atlantic Ocean. The difference in height between the Atlantic and Kingston at the mouth of Lake Ontario is 66m, so a series of locks raises and lowers ships. It now takes only eight to ten days for a large cargo ship to travel from Lake Superior into the Atlantic. Today the seaway provides jobs for 40,000 people and is one of the most important shipping lanes in the world. A

This paper mill at Thunder Bay on Lake Superior uses timber from the surrounding forests.

typical Great Lakes cargo ship, or "laker," carries 25,000 metric tons of cargo and is 222m long. To transport the same load by road or rail would require 600 trucks or 250 boxcars. The lakers carry mainly bulk cargoes, such as grain, iron ore and coal. There are huge grain storage facilities alongside the St Lawrence River where the grain can be kept until exported.

THE GREAT LAKES

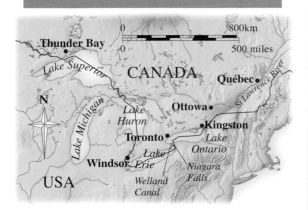

TRAFFIC BY COMMODITY, ST LAWRENCE SEAWAY, 2001

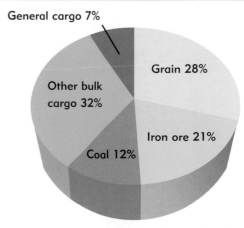

General cargo 7%
Grain 28%
Other bulk cargo 32%
Iron ore 21%
Coal 12%

Source: Transport Canada

People strolling along the attractive Inner Harbour area of Victoria, British Columbia.

THE STRUCTURE OF THE POPULATION

The population of Canada, like that of many developed nations, has a growing percentage of elderly people. In 1961, only 8 percent of Canadians were over 65 but by 1999 this had risen to 12 percent. By 2020, nearly 20 percent of the population is expected to be in this age group.

BIRTH RATE AND LIFE EXPECTANCY

Between 1945 (the end of World War II) and 1965 there was a huge increase in Canada's birth rate from 20.0 to 28.9 per 1,000 people. People born at that time, nicknamed "baby boomers," put heavy pressure on hospitals, schools and food supplies in the early years of their lives. Now, as they begin to reach retirement age, they will again place heavy demands on hospitals and on pension funds and care services. There has been an increase in average life expectancy. On average, a woman who was born in the early 1950s can expect to live to 71, while children born in 1996 have a life expectancy of 78 years.

The birth rate in Canada has fallen since the 1960s, and is now 10.99 per 1,000 people. If it were not for immigration, the population would start to decline in the next decade. Today Canadian women are having fewer children than in previous generations, and they are having their first child later. In the late 1990s, 33 percent of first births were to women over age 30.

LIFE EXPECTANCY AT BIRTH

Age

80
78
76
74
72
70
68
66
64

1960 1970 1980 1990 2000 2002

Source: Social Watch, 2004

UNDER-FIVE MORTALITY RATE

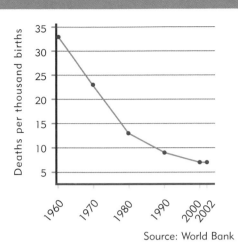

Source: World Bank

POPULATION DENSITY

PROVINCE	PEOPLE PER km²
Prince Edward Island	23.8
Nova Scotia	17.0
Ontario	12.5
New Brunswick	10.2
Quebec	5.2
Alberta	4.6
British Columbia	4.2
Manitoba	2.0
Saskatchewan	1.8
Newfoundland and Labrador	1.4
Yukon	0.2
Northwest Territory	0.1
Nunavut	0.1

Source: Statistics Canada

AN UNEVEN SPREAD OF PEOPLE

Most of Canada's population live within 200km of the US border, with 60 percent living in just two provinces – Ontario and Quebec. Even within these provinces the population is greatest in the southern areas toward the US border, around the port cities of the Great Lakes and the St Lawrence River.

The Atlantic provinces, which include Newfoundland and Labrador, New Brunswick, Prince Edward Island, and Nova Scotia, are quite densely populated although their total populations are not large. The largest settlements are again in port cities, such as Halifax. But the area as a whole is beginning to show signs of depopulation, as it is away from the core regions near the US border. It tends to be the younger, educated members of the population who migrate to the core region to look for better jobs. This can produce an unbalanced population in some settlements, with mainly the older people remaining. Eventually this can lead to the closure of facilities, such as schools, which makes the area even less attractive to families and adds to the decline.

Manitoba, Saskatchewan and Alberta – the Prairie provinces – are mainly rural and agricultural. Most of the population live in cities, such as Winnipeg, Regina and Calgary.

With a population of just over 4 million, British Columbia is the third-most populous province after Ontario and Quebec. More than half of its people live in Vancouver. This city has important links with the countries of the Pacific Rim, such as Japan and China, and is continuing to expand.

The northern territories – Nunavut, the Northwest Territories and Yukon – form 41 percent of Canada's landmass but have only 0.3 percent of the population, a total of 102,400 people. Most people live in the administrative centers, such as Yellowknife, or in small settlements linked to mining or oil extraction. There is some limited growth in population, but winters that last eight months do not attract large numbers of people to the region.

POPULATION 1950–2050

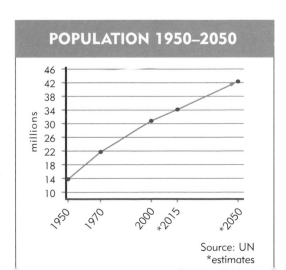

Source: UN
*estimates

THE IMPACT OF IMMIGRATION

Around 15,000 years ago, sea levels were much lower than today and Siberia in Asia and Alaska were joined by a land bridge. People migrated from Asia into North America, following herds of caribou that were their main source of food. These were the people who formed the Indian tribes of Canada who are today known as the First Nations.

EARLY EUROPEANS

In the sixteenth century, the French settled in eastern Canada to create New France. Later, in the sixteenth and seventeenth centuries, they were joined by the English, who eventually took over Canada. After 1763 the French were not driven out but were allowed to stay, and many held on to their different beliefs and way of life. Today Canadians think of their country as a "mosaic" of peoples rather than expecting everyone to conform to the same way of life.

A busy street in Toronto's Chinatown.

Pier 21 in Halifax, Nova Scotia – the original gateway for immigrants to Canada.

LATER MIGRATIONS

In the eighteenth century, after their defeat by the English at Culloden, many Scots migrated to Canada, and thousands of Irish people arrived after the potato famine in the nineteenth century. Today, 60 percent of Canadians can trace their ancestors back to Britain or Ireland.

In the late nineteenth century, as a result of persecution, and again after the creation of the USSR, there were migrations of Ukrainians who settled mainly in the Prairie provinces, where their distinctive culture survives to this day. Italians and Germans came in the late nineteenth century and again after World War II to escape poverty. Immigrants still arrive in Canada from southern Italy, but in much smaller numbers. The first large migration of Chinese people was in the 1850s, when many found work building the roads and railways that opened up the west of Canada.

CASE STUDY:
THE FUJIAN BOAT PEOPLE

In 1999, four ships carrying 600 illegal passengers were stopped off Canada's west coast. The poorly prepared vessels had taken 39 days to cross the Pacific Ocean. Their passengers were mainly unskilled workers from the Chinese coastal region of Fujian, who had paid large sums of money to be taken to Canada in the belief that they would have a much better life there. After being held for a year, only 4 percent of them (24 out of the 600) were allowed to stay. Of the Chinese who applied through the usual legal channels that year, 58 percent were accepted.

With its falling birth rate, Canada needs migrants to come and fill the gaps in its workforce, but it needs people with skills and education.

IMMIGRATION TODAY

Although there is still some migration from Europe, it is mainly from eastern European countries such as Romania and Albania. The largest numbers of immigrants now come

Montreal is a cosmopolitan city with people from many ethnic groups.

from Asia. In Vancouver, on the Pacific coast, 56 percent of immigrants are of Asian origin. Most immigrants (48 percent) are between 24 and 44 years old, and a quarter have college degrees. They are skilled workers, many being engineers, computer specialists and scientists. Of the 250,346 immigrants who moved to Canada in 2001, 11 percent were refugees from war zones, who were given loans to help them get started in their new country. The most popular destination for immigrants is the province of Ontario, which is the heart of the Canadian economy.

IMMIGRANTS' ORIGINS (AS PERCENTAGE OF TOTAL) BEFORE 1961 AND 1991–2001

BEFORE 1961

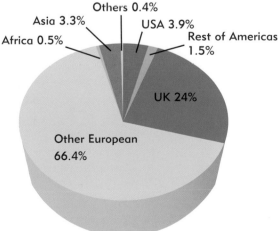

Others 0.4%
Asia 3.3%
Africa 0.5%
USA 3.9%
Rest of Americas 1.5%
UK 24%
Other European 66.4%

1991–2001

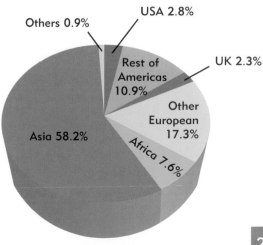

Others 0.9%
USA 2.8%
Rest of Americas 10.9%
UK 2.3%
Other European 17.3%
Africa 7.6%
Asia 58.2%

Source: Statistics Canada

23

French café culture in Quebec City.

THE FRENCH CONNECTION

Quebec is known by its French-speaking inhabitants as La Belle Province, "the beautiful province." It is the second-largest province by population, with more than 7 million people. Almost a quarter of Canadians speak French as their first language and 85 percent of these French-speakers live in Quebec.

The Québecois, the people who live in Quebec, view themselves as different from most Canadians. This is partly because French is their main language and also because their culture reflects their French origins.

EARLY SETTLERS

The French were the first to settle this part of Canada and they founded its capital, Quebec City, in 1608. They were attracted to Canada by the abundance of animals that could be hunted for their skins, including elk, bear and beaver. Settlements sprang up to provide provisions for hunters and to act as markets for the furs they brought out of the north and west. Quebec was an important port for the export of these resources. French people also settled in other provinces, such as Nova Scotia and New Brunswick, where they concentrated on fishing and some agriculture.

Once the British took over Canada in the eighteenth century, some of the French moved into the United States, but the majority in Quebec stayed and were allowed to continue with their French traditions.

MODERN QUEBEC

Today the French language and culture are flourishing. French is one of the two national languages of Canada and all information and signs must be in both English and French. Although a European French-speaker would understand the French Canadian language, there are differences in accent and vocabulary.

LEFT: The French-style Chateau Frontenac is Quebec's most famous landmark.

ABOVE: A bilingual street sign in French and English, showing parking restrictions.

BELOW: Jacques Cartier Square in Vieux (Old) Montreal, an attractive historic area within the modern city.

Joual, a dialect of Quebec, is a mix of French, slang and some English. Young people use it because they find it more expressive than the usual French Canadian, and often adults don't know what it means.

Although Montreal is larger, Quebec City is the capital of the province and has a population of about 750,000. It is the heart of French Canadian nationalism – a movement that would like to see Quebec as an independent country.

SEPARATISM

In the 1960s and 1970s there was a feeling that French language and culture were declining and a new political party – the Parti Québecois – set out to create a separate French-speaking country. Quebec is three times the size of France and has a strong economy. The Parti Québecois asserts that it could survive as an independent country and therefore protect French language and culture in North America. In 1995, the Canadian people voted on whether Quebec should be a separate country. The majority (50.6 percent) voted to keep it in Canada but most French-speaking Canadians feel that their culture and language are so distinct that Quebec should stand alone.

THE FIRST NATIONS

The first people to live in Canada arrived from Asia many thousands of years ago. Today they are known in Canada as the First Nations and they include tribes such as the Mohawk, who originally settled near the St Lawrence River, and the Blackfeet, who lived and hunted on the Great Plains. The Inuit, who settled in the far north, came from a different ethnic grouping but are sometimes included in the term First Nations.

CHANGING FORTUNES

The First Nations saw themselves as part of nature. They took from nature only what they needed, which was opposite to the Europeans' goal of extracting as much as they could in order to make money. The lives of the First Nations completely changed with the coming of Europeans to Canada from the sixteenth century onward. The Europeans competed for resources and, over the years, took the tribes' lands from them, allowing them to continue living only on reserved land set aside by the government. Native languages and cultures were repressed.

Today, the First Nations have a population of nearly 1 million and are once again taking

A Cree Indian woman in northern Quebec province cleaning a caribou skin. Caribou are used to provide food, clothing and shelter for First Nation peoples.

control of their language, culture and traditions. In 1982, the Assembly of First Nations was formed, which aims for peaceful coexistence and a more equal sharing of land and resources within Canada. The Assembly helped set up the territory of Nunavut for the Inuit people.

NUNAVUT – CANADA'S NEWEST TERRITORY

On 1 April 1999, the self-governing territory of Nunavut (meaning "Our Land") was created. It is a homeland for the Inuit people and is now largely responsible for decisions about its future development. It still receives considerable financial help from the federal government in Ottawa. Covering a fifth of Canada's landmass, Nunavut has a population of only 29,000, 85 percent of whom are Inuit. Its capital, Iqaluit on Baffin Island, has a population of just 6,000. The Inuit language of Inuktitut has replaced English as the official language of the territory.

The region has traditionally supported itself by harvesting natural resources such as seal fur, whale meat and blubber, and fish. This brings in about Can$40 million each year. More recently, mineral exploration and extraction have become much more important: They earn more than Can$300 million a year. This part of the economy is growing and will provide much of the income for Nunavut for years to come. Tourism is also growing and the territory now attracts about 18,000 visitors a year. Some arrive at Baffin Island in cruise ships, but many others go for ecotours, to view the wilderness areas and the wildlife.

There are many challenges facing the new territory, including the fact that its infrastructure (which includes roads, ports, airports, water and sewage facilities) is poorly developed. It is difficult and expensive to establish services such as schools and medical centers for widely scattered communities because the transportation networks are poor. Most electricity is generated by burning diesel fuel, which has to be imported into the region during the short summer and then stored in tanks over the winter when deliveries are impossible.

An Inuit mother and daughter prepare Arctic char (a salmonlike fish) for drying and preserving.

Information technology (IT) is seen as important in developing such scattered communities, and knowledge of IT is being encouraged within the newly developed Inuit school curriculum. The idea is for students to have a balance between knowledge and understanding of Inuit culture and language and preparation to help them take their place within Canada's new knowledge-based industries.

A street scene in Baker Lake, Nunavut, where parked Ski-Doos have replaced cars.

LIFE AND LEISURE

Canada has a high standard of living and, in terms of purchasing power, is second only to the United States. There is a well-established system of social security that acts as a safety net when things go wrong (such as a period of unemployment) but this means that taxation levels are high.

EDUCATION

Health and education are organized by the government of each province, with some of the money coming from the federal government of Canada. Canadian students can follow a course of study that will eventually lead to university or a program that is more relevant to a specific job, such as plumber or draftsperson. They can also choose to study a mix of practical and academic courses. After secondary school, students can take higher courses related to a specific career, such as nursing, in a community college. There are more than 200 such colleges in Canada, and students tend to go to the one nearest their home. The country also has 75 universities, some of which are world famous, including the University of Toronto and McGill University in Montreal.

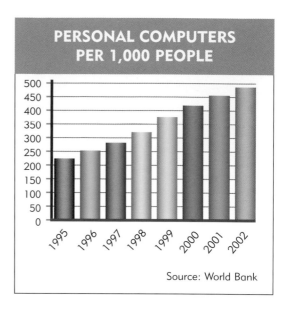

PERSONAL COMPUTERS PER 1,000 PEOPLE

Source: World Bank

MEDIA

Most adults read a newspaper at some time during the week. There are many provincial papers, such as the conservative tabloid *The Vancouver Sun*, but there are two important national papers – *The National Post* and *The Globe and Mail*. *Le Devoir* is the French-language paper based in Quebec. Magazine sales are high, and although many magazines are from the United States, the most popular woman's title, *Châtelaine*, is Canadian.

Canadians have access to a wide range of TV channels including more than 40 channels delivered via cable. The Canadian Broadcasting Company (CBC) is funded by the federal government. There are three other large TV networks, including one in the French language. There are also many regional channels, including news channels in both English and French.

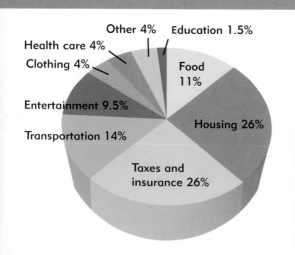

AVERAGE HOUSEHOLD EXPENDITURE, 2002 (% OF TOTAL)

Other 4%
Education 1.5%
Health care 4%
Clothing 4%
Food 11%
Entertainment 9.5%
Transportation 14%
Housing 26%
Taxes and insurance 26%

Source: Statistics Canada

TELECOMMUNICATIONS DATA (PER 1,000 PEOPLE)

Mainline Phones	635
Mobile Phones	377
Internet Users	513

Source: World Bank

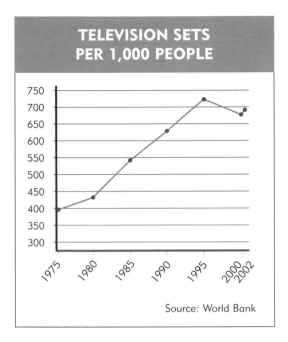

TELEVISION SETS PER 1,000 PEOPLE

Source: World Bank

Music fans at a concert at Wasaga Beach, Ontario, in the summer of 2004.

MUSIC AND SPORTS

Canadian music covers a wide range from pop to folk to rock and jazz. Canadian artists of world renown include Leonard Cohen, Joni Mitchell, Alanis Morissette, Shania Twain and Celine Dion.

Playing and watching sports are an important part of Canadian life. Ice hockey is the most popular sport and is widely played; almost every town has an ice hockey rink. The National Hockey League (NHL) was set up in 1917 and the most important prize is the Stanley Cup. However, lacrosse is Canada's national sport, even though it is less popular than ice hockey. Invented by the First Nations, lacrosse involves throwing and catching a ball with a small leather cradle at the end of a stick.

Baseball and basketball are increasingly popular in Canada. Basketball, although developed in the United States, was invented by a Canadian. Some Canadian teams, such as the Toronto Raptors, have made it into the National Basketball Association, the world's top professional league.

Canada hosts two important golf tournaments each year – the Canadian Open and the Greater Vancouver Open. Golf is increasing in popularity and there are nearly 2,000 golf courses in the country.

Winter sports, including skiing and snowboarding, take place in the Rocky Mountains. Ski resorts, such as Whistler, are relatively new but are now attracting Europeans to their uncrowded slopes.

Canadians enjoy the outdoors that their country provides. Hiking, biking, fishing, canoeing and camping are all popular pastimes. Thousands of Canadian students attend a wide variety of camps organized during the summer vacation. Some are based on a specific activity, such as canoeing, while others are more general outdoor activity camps.

An unusual regatta at Windsor, Nova Scotia, with racers navigating pumpkins.

A view of Toronto's skyline from the observation deck of the CN Tower.

CITIES OF THE EAST

The cities of the east grew because of good transport networks, especially links via the St Lawrence River and the Great Lakes to the interior of Canada. Goods coming out from the center of Canada, such as furs, wheat and coal, could be transferred onto ships for export to Europe. Today Toronto and Montreal are the two largest cities in Canada, and they continue to attract migrants from all parts of the world.

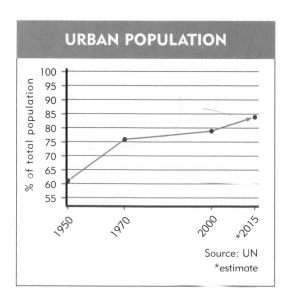

URBAN POPULATION

Source: UN
*estimate

The city of Ottawa is in the same region as Toronto and Montreal, and it became Canada's capital as a compromise: Toronto was seen as too English, and Montreal and Quebec as too French. Ottawa has the Parliament Buildings and many important museums. More than 90 percent of the city's labor force works in service industries and it has an important area of high-technology industries.

Other important cities include the port of Halifax in Nova Scotia and St John's in Newfoundland. Halifax was the point of entry for many of Canada's migrants and refugees. The port of St John's, whose industry was traditionally fishing, is now an important base for oil exploration.

TORONTO

Toronto is the largest city in Canada and is its chief industrial center, producing a quarter of Canada's manufactured output. Although founded originally by the French, it was taken over by the British who set up the street grid, which influenced the modern layout of the city. During the nineteenth century, Toronto was referred to as "The Big Smoke" because of the air pollution caused by the large number of factories built there. Today its most important manufacturing sector is linked to the car industry. Toronto is also the main financial center of Canada, with an important stock exchange.

Toronto has become less important as a port, and much of the harbor area has recently been redeveloped to provide upscale apartments, hotels and landscaped green spaces. Toronto is a cosmopolitan city with a variety of very successful sectors in both manufacturing and service industries.

MONTREAL

Montreal, Canada's second city, is located 1,600km inland from the Atlantic Ocean and has been an important port since the arrival of European settlers. It is a road and rail hub and has good access to the Great Lakes and to the Atlantic. It is a large container port as well as a port of call for cruise ships. Since World War II there has been a rapid decline in its older, labor-intensive industries, especially textiles, but this has been balanced by a growth in science-based industries. Montreal's well-educated population, and the world-class research carried out at McGill University, have attracted aeronautics and telecommunications companies to the city. About 66 percent of the Province of Quebec's income is generated in Montreal. The city is also important culturally, especially for the French-speakers who make up 70 percent of its population. Montreal has many museums and hosts international events and festivals, including the world-famous Montreal Jazz Festival.

ETHNIC COMPOSITION OF TORONTO AND MONTREAL, 2001 (% OF POPULATION)

	TORONTO	MONTREAL
White	63.0	86.2
Asian	24.0	5.3
Black	7.1	4.2
Arab	2.2	2.3
South American	1.6	1.6
Other	2.1	0.4

Source: Adapted from Statistics Canada

The city has harsh winters, and to help combat this there is an underground shopping zone under the city center. This idea began in 1900 when one store company linked two sites with an underground tunnel. Today there are 27km of underground walkways linking 50 buildings including shops, department stores, hotels, offices and five subway stations.

Shoppers buying flowers from a stall in Montreal's underground city.

FROM EAST TO WEST

North and west of Canada's core region is the thinly populated Canadian Shield. The area's forests and poor soils acted as a barrier to settlement. The regions farther west were not settled in any major way until the late nineteenth century, when transcontinental railway lines were built that opened up areas to the west of the Great Lakes. European migrants were eager to settle the fertile lands they found beyond the Canadian Shield, which became the Prairie provinces of Manitoba, Saskatchewan and Alberta. Towns grew up alongside the railroad and acted as supply posts for the new farmers and as export points for the grain and cattle they produced.

CASE STUDY
CALGARY

ABOVE: A rider demonstrates his skills in front of crowds at the Calgary Stampede, held every July.

The city of Calgary began as a frontier outpost when the western Plains were first settled. It benefited from being close to one of the few passes through the Rocky Mountains that the railway could be built through. Once the railway was up and running, the city grew steadily.

Today Calgary is one of the fastest-growing cities in Canada and is an important center for the wheat and oil industries. Although much of the oil reserves are found farther to the north, most oil company headquarters are located in Calgary. This in turn has attracted e-commerce and electronics companies to the area, contributing to the rapid growth of the city.

Alongside a growing tourist industry (Calgary is the major access point for Banff and its associated national parks), oil, finance and high-tech industries, the traditional industries of grain and beef production continue to play an important role within the city's economy.

The city of Winnipeg developed as a rail export point for Prairie grain. Industries such as food processing and farm machinery manufacturing grew in response to the needs of the region, and the city contains over half the population of the province of Manitoba.

Farther west, other major settlements such as Regina and Edmonton grew up, initially as agricultural and administrative centers. Oil became a major resource in the Edmonton region and is an important component in its industry. The city is also known as "The Gateway to the North" and has links to many of the far-flung settlements of the Yukon and Northwest Territories.

VANCOUVER

Vancouver is Canada's main port – handling 75 million tons of cargo a year – and is also its fastest growing city. It processes and exports much of the resources of British Columbia, its leading industries being food processing and timber products. Vancouver has very good links with the countries of the Pacific Rim, including China, Japan and South Korea, and has a sizable population of Asian origin. Nearly 30 percent of the city's population aged 25 or over has a university degree, compared with 17 percent for Canada as a whole.

Sulfur awaiting shipment next to a container ship in Vancouver harbor.

The city is a pleasant place to live and to visit, with its backdrop of mountains, excellent beaches and many urban green spaces, including the 404 hectares of Stanley Park near the center of the city.

The wide variety of foods available provides a tempting display at Granville Island's market in Vancouver.

ETHNIC COMPOSITION OF CALGARY AND VANCOUVER, 2001 (% OF POPULATION)

	CALGARY	VANCOUVER
White	82.9	63.0
Asian	13.0	32.8
Black	1.4	1.0
Arab	1.2	1.4
South American	0.9	1.0
Other	0.6	0.8

Source: Adapted from Statistics Canada

AGRICULTURE

A farmer sprays a potato field in Park Corner, Prince Edward Island.

Canada's farming area is about the size of the state of Texas, but this is only 7 percent of Canada's total landmass. Its main agricultural export is wheat, grown mainly in the three Prairie provinces of Manitoba, Saskatchewan and Alberta. It is durum wheat, which is especially good for bread and pasta making. Even Italy imports large quantities of Canadian wheat for pasta making.

AGRICULTURAL DIVERSITY

Canada has fewer farms today than in the mid-twentieth century, but they are larger. Agriculture currently contributes about 2.3 percent of the country's GDP. Although wheat is important, Canada also produces large quantities of good-quality beef and vegetable oils. Apples are the largest fruit crop and potatoes are the most valuable vegetable crop; both flourish in the cool climates of Canada.

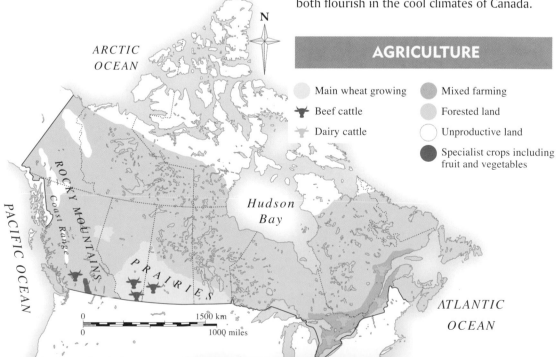

AGRICULTURE

- Main wheat growing
- Beef cattle
- Dairy cattle
- Mixed farming
- Forested land
- Unproductive land
- Specialist crops including fruit and vegetables

ARCTIC OCEAN

N

ROCKY MOUNTAINS
Coast Range

PACIFIC OCEAN

Hudson Bay

PRAIRIES

ATLANTIC OCEAN

0   1500 km
0   1000 miles

There are also more than 10,000 maple syrup producers; the syrup is an important ingredient in Canadian cooking (see page 41).

In Canada, as in much of the developed world, farmers are diversifying – trying different ways of making money from their land. Farm incomes have been falling since the mid-1990s new products are being tried such as llamas, wild boar and ostriches. The native bison is now farmed commercially, with more than 100,000 raised on farms for meat.

Farming is now less intensive than it once was. Farmers have come to realize that growing the same crop year after year, and relying on large amounts of chemical fertilizers and pesticides, harms the very environment on which they depend.

FARMING IN THE EAST

In the Atlantic region of Canada, farms are generally small. The soils tend to be poor and thin, the landscape is hilly and the harsh climate is not ideal for large-scale commercial crop growing. However, there are some areas of better soils in the lowlands, especially on Prince Edward Island, where the main potato-growing region is located.

In the core region of Ontario and Quebec, the lowland soils are fertile and the climate is milder, particularly in the south of the region.

Rounding up cattle in southern Alberta. Beef production is still important in this area.

Most of the agricultural products in Ontario and Quebec are of high value, including peaches, raspberries, strawberries and honey. Ontario has mixed farming but the farms are small scale. Apart from some dairying and wheat farming, specialist crops such as tobacco, fruit and sugar beet are grown. Quebec is farther north and has a cooler climate better suited to dairying, although it also produces 82 percent of Canada's maple syrup crop.

THE PRAIRIES

Farther west, the relatively low rainfall of the Prairie provinces favors cereal growing, and 17 percent of the world's wheat is grown there. Large areas of generally flat land and fertile soil helped establish large-scale wheat farming in the region, although this is now changing.

THE WEST

Much of western Canada is too mountainous to support agriculture, though there are small lowland areas and valleys where specialist farming occurs. One such is the Okanagan Valley in the Rockies, where there is a sunny and relatively dry climate ideal for orchards and vineyards. Known as "The Golden Mile," the valley contains 9,000 hectares of the most productive land in Canada, and nine major wineries are based there.

Farther west, on the narrow lowland plains of the Vancouver region, mild winters and plentiful rainfall support dairying and fruit growing for the large market of the city.

CONTRIBUTION TO FARM INCOME BY PRODUCT

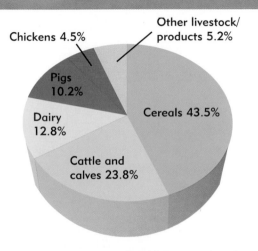

Chickens 4.5%
Other livestock/products 5.2%
Pigs 10.2%
Dairy 12.8%
Cereals 43.5%
Cattle and calves 23.8%

Source: Statistics Canada

A grain elevator at Nanton, Alberta. Although most are no longer in use, several elevators are being preserved as historical buildings.

CHANGE ON THE PRAIRIES

The Canadian Prairies – the provinces of Manitoba, Saskatchewan and Alberta – form the northern section of the Great Plains, which extend as far south as Texas in the United States. With their fertile brown and black soils they are an important agricultural region and are known as the "Breadbasket of the World" because of the huge amount of wheat grown there. The Prairies were opened up to commercial farming only in 1885 with the coming of the Canadian Pacific Railway.

The farming is extensive, meaning that the levels of chemical and labor input are low per hectare, even though large quantities of wheat, beef and oils are produced. The chemical inputs, such as fertilizers, are lower per hectare than in Europe and the crop yields are correspondingly lower, but land is plentiful so production totals from the region are high.

PROBLEMS OF THE REGION

Although wheat was grown in most suitable areas of the Prairies in the middle of the twentieth century, more recently there has been a move away from concentration on just this one product. This is a result of a number of problems that have faced Prairie farmers. Although the soils are mainly fertile, rainfall is low because the region is in the rain shadow of the Rockies, and drought can be a problem. When the Prairie soils dry out they are susceptible to soil erosion, especially by the wind. The problem can be reduced if farmers follow soil conservation methods – including zero tillage, the technique of planting seeds for the next crop without disturbing the soil by ploughing. They can also leave part of their land fallow (unused) every year to allow its fertility to build up.

Climatic hazards in the region include violent hailstorms, which can flatten crops, and harsh frosts. The frosts mean that wheat can be sown only in spring to avoid the worst of the cold. This results in a shorter growing season, and special varieties of spring wheat are used to cope with this.

A newer problem is bovine spongiform encephalopathy (BSE), or "mad cow disease." In 2003 BSE was found in Alberta, in a single cow that had originated in the United Kingdom. Canada's beef export market crashed and the price per animal fell 98 percent. Although the United States was again importing Canadian beef by 2004, Canada's important markets in South Korea and Japan have not recovered and farmers' incomes suffered badly.

In an effort to generate income and to try to combat their multiple problems, farmers are trying a range of new ideas. For those near an urban area, agrotourism is one possible solution. This involves organizing farm tours for which people pay, or having paying guests stay on the farm. Other ideas are bison and elk ranching, and growing organic crops, herbs and spices. There is also a growing demand for greenhouse crops, such as tomatoes, peppers and cucumbers, especially near larger settlements.

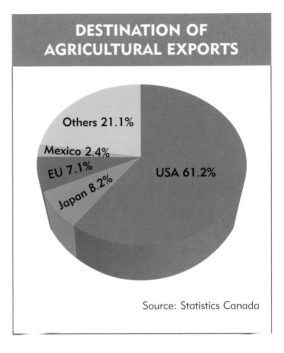

DESTINATION OF AGRICULTURAL EXPORTS

Others 21.1%

Mexico 2.4%

EU 7.1%

Japan 8.2%

USA 61.2%

Source: Statistics Canada

As older farmers approach retirement age, their children are choosing not to take over and many farms are up for sale. However, it looks as if the future will favor the large farms that have the money to invest in new ideas and expensive machinery. Many large farms are owned by agribusinesses, usually a combination of finance and agricultural management companies.

Harvesting wheat on Saskatchewan's open prairie fields.

RESOURCES

A worker holding a lump of oil sand which, when heated, produces useable oil.

anada is rich in many mineral resources, including iron ore, uranium and fossil fuels. Around 80 percent of mined metals and other minerals are exported, and in 2001 they formed 12.6 percent of the country's exports.

FOSSIL FUEL RESOURCES

Canada is an important coal producer and it exports nearly half of all that is mined within its borders. Most is mined in Alberta, which also has important gas and oil reserves.

Much of Canada's coal is lignite (brown coal) that is dug out of the ground in huge open-cast pits. The material on top of the coal seam is removed using machines called draglines, some of which weigh 3,000 to 5,000 tonnes. Then huge mechanical shovels are used to dig out the coal. Demand for coal, especially lignite, is falling because of the pollution produced when it is burned.

FOSSIL FUELS AND MINERALS

Key	
Gas	Fe Iron ore
Oil	Cu Copper
Lignite	P Potash
Coal	Zn Zinc
	D Diamonds
	U Uranium

ARCTIC OCEAN

N

Norman Wells
Fe

Lac de Gras
D

Hudson Bay

PACIFIC OCEAN

U U Cu

Fort McMurray U
Rabbit Lake

Zn Cu Zn

P

Cu

Sudbury Cu
Fe

Cu

Fe

Cu

500 km
1000 miles

ATLANTIC OCEAN

Sudbury, a town in central Ontario, is known as "Nickel City" and is the center of Canada's largest mining region. Over the last 100 years, the mining and processing of minerals have caused soil and water pollution. Very little would grow in the highly acidic soils, and the nearby lakes had little life in them.

Some of the problems have been solved by fitting filters to factory chimneys to remove pollutants, spraying local lakes with lime to reduce acidity, planting large numbers of trees to reduce the flow of polluted runoff water and creating reed beds around polluted mining ponds to absorb many of the polluting chemicals. Grasses are now beginning to grow on the previously polluted land, and fish such as trout are reappearing in the rivers and lakes.

Oil and gas are found in Saskatchewan and the Northwest Territories, as well as in Alberta and off the coasts of the Atlantic provinces. The Mackenzie delta in the Northwest Territories has large gas and oil reserves but the area is also very important for migrating wildfowl and caribou herds. Studies have shown that the development of oil and gas reserves in the region has reduced the numbers of wildlife because of the disturbance it causes.

A newer source of oil – oil sands – is being exploited in places such as Fort McMurray in northern Alberta. This is a mixture of thick oil and sand that is dug up and heated, releasing the oil which is then piped off.

MINERALS

Many minerals are found within the ancient rocks of the Canadian Shield but there are other important deposits elsewhere. Canada leads the world in the production of uranium, which is the fuel for nuclear power stations, and exports 85 percent of what is mined. The richest deposits are found in the province of Saskatchewan, in locations such as Rabbit Lake.

Canada is also the leading producer of potash, with 33 percent of the world's supply. Potash is mainly used in the manufacture of fertilizer, and huge quantities are transported by rail to export ports such as Thunder Bay on Lake Superior.

In the late twentieth century, Canada's first diamond mine was opened near Lac de Gras in the Northwest Territories. When fully operational it will produce 5 percent of the world's diamonds.

Metal ore deposits are also important in Canada and there are still good reserves of iron ore, nickel, lead and copper, as well as antimony and zinc.

A potash mine in New Brunswick. Huge boring machines drill out the mineral which is then carried to the surface by conveyor belt.

A small fishing vessel in Port au Choix, Newfoundland. Overfishing has made it hard for small fishing businesses to survive.

FISHING

Canada has had some of the most productive fishing grounds in the world, especially off the Grand Banks on the east coast and off the coasts of British Columbia in the west. However, since the 1950s there has been a great deal of overfishing on the Grand Banks. Cod stocks have fallen so low that most cod

REASONS FOR THE FAILURE OF COD STOCKS

- Introduction of large-scale factory ships that catch thousands of tons at a time.
- Overfishing – catching young fish before they reach maturity.
- Increase in the seal population due to the decline in fur trade. Seals eat fish.
- Damage to spawning grounds caused by heavy trawl nets raking the seabed habitat.
- Reduction in numbers of the smaller fish that the cod feed on.

fishing was banned in the mid-1990s. Even so, by 2004 the numbers of cod had still not increased. Around 40,000 people have lost some or all of their income because of the decline of the cod, and fishermen have left the Atlantic provinces to find work elsewhere. On the west coast, salmon stocks are also falling. Fish farming is being developed as an alternative to deep-sea fishing and, if successful, it may provide employment for fishing communities.

FUR

The fur trade was one of the reasons that Canada was first settled by Europeans, but the amount earned by this industry has fallen as attitudes to wearing animal skins have changed. However, there is still a demand for fur from the fashion industry and from the countries of Scandinavia.

Of the fur produced in Canada, 53 percent is farmed and 47 percent is from animals trapped in the wild. Mink accounts for 90 percent of farmed fur, while muskrat and beaver are the most common wild pelts. Controversy surrounds the annual killing of baby harp seals, as they are normally clubbed to death to avoid damaging their white pelts. Television and press pictures of this practice led to a decline in demand, and harp seal numbers grew rapidly. By 2004, there were so many that wildlife authorities permitted a cull of 350,000 seals over an eight-week period. The growth in seal numbers is seen as a problem because fishermen blame the seals (rather than overfishing) for reducing fish catches.

FORESTS

Canada's forests cover nearly half of the country and are a significant part of the economy. One in every 17 jobs is linked to forestry. About 4 percent of the forests are harvested each year, with British Columbia providing the most timber and timber products. There are more than 150 different species of tree, 80 percent being softwoods such as hemlock, spruce and Douglas fir. Tree replanting now plays a major

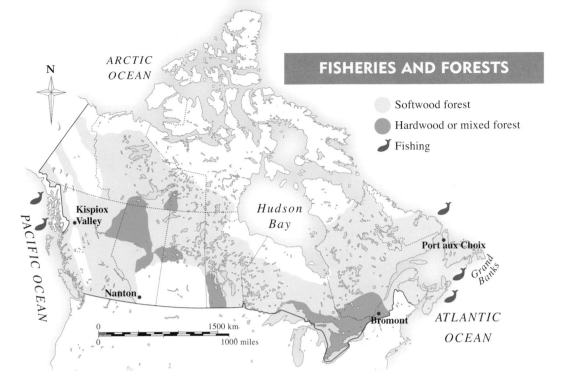

Softwood forest
Hardwood or mixed forest
Fishing

ARCTIC OCEAN

N

PACIFIC OCEAN

Kispiox Valley

Nanton

Hudson Bay

Port aux Choix

Grand Banks

Bromont

ATLANTIC OCEAN

0   1500 km
0   1000 miles

role in timber production as the industry tries to operate in a sustainable way by replacing the resources it takes.

There are many threats to Canada's forests apart from the logging itself. In 2002, 2.8 million hectares were seriously damaged by forest fires and a further 19 million hectares by insect damage. Both these threats seem to be increasing, perhaps as a result of global warming. Acid rain is causing widespread damage in the east of the country as industrial and vehicle emissions from Ontario's industries and cities dissolve in the rain, which then falls on the forests farther east.

CASE STUDY
MAPLE SYRUP PRODUCTION

Canada produces 85 percent of the world's maple syrup, which is used as a topping on ice cream and pancakes as well as in other desserts. A harvester "taps" the sugar maple tree by cutting holes into its bark, allowing the sap to run out. The sap is then collected in a container. Although maple sap has a very distinctive flavor it is 97 percent water and has to be concentrated. It takes 45 liters of sap to make 1 liter of syrup. There are 10,300 maple syrup producers, mostly in Quebec, and in 2002 they produced 35,000 tonnes of syrup.

A worker in Quebec drills into the bark of a sugar maple tree to collect the sap.

41

A logger in British Columbia working for Interfor, one of western Canada's largest logging and lumber milling companies.

Much of Canada's manufacturing industry is based on the rich resources found within its borders, such as the paper, pulp, and timber industries; steel production; food processing; and flour milling. Most industrial manufacturing (40 percent) is based in the three largest urban regions of Toronto, Montreal and Vancouver, and it is within these three cities that most company headquarters are found.

MANUFACTURING INDUSTRY

Toronto has a large number of car and car parts factories to supply both the Canadian and US markets. Japanese car companies build cars in Canada for export to the United States, because this avoids the heavy US import taxes that would be levied on shipments from Japan. Exports are vital to most Canadian industries because, at less than 32 million people, Canada's domestic market is quite small.

Advanced Manufacturing Technology (AMT) is the use of computer-controlled systems in industrial processes such as the molding of plastics and metal cutting and machining.

An assembly-line worker checks a vehicle door at a Honda car plant near Toronto.

ECONOMIC STRUCTURE, 2003 (% GDP CONTRIBUTIONS)

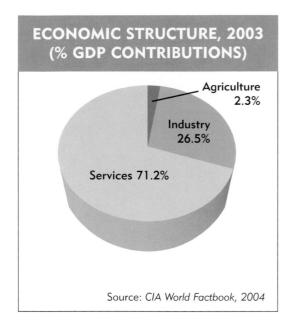

Agriculture 2.3%

Industry 26.5%

Services 71.2%

Source: *CIA World Factbook, 2004*

GNI PER CAPITA (US$)

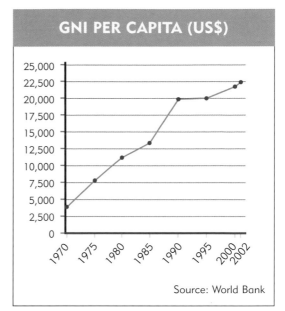

Source: World Bank

This computer-aided technology is important in the car industry, especially around Ontario. Long term, AMT will probably mean fewer workers will be needed although industries will become more efficient. Producing goods more cheaply means that companies are more able to compete in the global marketplace.

Canada's labor-intensive textile industries were based in Montreal. As these industries have declined because of cheaper competition from the Far East, other industries, such as aerospace, have become more important.

Bearing in mind the importance of food production in Canada, it is not surprising that food-processing industries are also important. They range from the milling of wheat to fish processing and the production of frozen dinners and frozen vegetables. Advanced technologies, such as automated quality testing and the use of ultrasound to kill harmful bacteria, are now used to help food preservation.

Small companies are important in Canada's manufacturing industry. Firms employing fewer than 200 workers are responsible for about 57 percent of all workers and for 40 percent of goods produced.

FEMALE LABOR FORCE (% OF TOTAL)

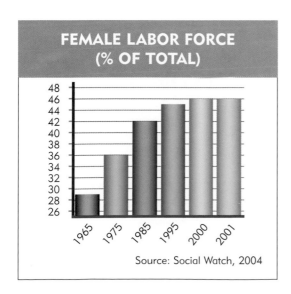

Source: Social Watch, 2004

CASE STUDY
ALUMINUM SMELTING IN KITIMAT

In 1950 the Nechako River was diverted to produce HEP for an aluminum smelting plant owned by Alcan in the isolated community of Kitimat in British Columbia. Kitimat is what is called a "company town" – one that has grown largely because of a single company operating there. Today, as a result of global competition, the Alcan plant is not operating at full capacity, and the future of Kitimat is uncertain. If the plant were to close, it would devastate the local economy because Alcan employs about 2,500 people locally. Kitimat now plans to diversify into other industries in order to provide a secure employment base for its residents.

EMPLOYMENT BY SECTOR, 2003

Primary industry	4%
Manufacturing/construction	21%
Service industry	75%

Source: Statistics Canada

Traders on the floor of the Montreal Stock Exchange.

SERVICE INDUSTRIES

Most people in Canada now work in service industries, including banking, insurance, public services such as education, the storage and transportation of goods, and retailing. Toronto and Montreal have the main stock exchanges, while Calgary is also an important financial center.

HIGH-TECH INDUSTRIES

Canada leads the world in many aspects of high technology, including robotics, fiber optics and biotechnology (making chemical products using living organisms). A high-tech zone known as Silicon Valley North has developed around Ottawa. This cluster of high-tech companies has grown up for a number of reasons. Ottawa is the capital of Canada, and the national government has invested in the development of computer systems. Also, there is a high level of research and development going on in both of the region's world-class universities and in its science laboratories and defense

establishments. The fruits of this research can be used by local high-tech businesses, and, in turn, many of the businesses provide funding for continued research. There is also access to investment money and a large pool of qualified workers – 35 percent of the population of Ottawa over age 25 have a university degree, compared with a national average of 17 percent.

High-technology companies are also located elsewhere in Canada, such as in Vancouver, and high-tech industries may provide employment in areas where traditional industries are in decline. One example of this is Newfoundland, where the fishing industry has all but collapsed and there is little other work available. The province has attracted notice as an area for growth and some high-tech companies are establishing themselves near the port city of St John's. Part of the appeal of the area is lower-cost labor and access to good research and development centers.

Canada invests heavily in research because it wishes to stay ahead in the field of technology. One new area of development is nanotechnology. This field involves the creation of new materials and devices that are so small they are at the molecular scale – about one billionth of a meter. Advances in nanotechnology will lead to much greater miniaturization of semiconductors and the computers in which they are used. Canada has set up a National Institute for Nanotechnology to investigate this field.

A high-tech company employee at work in a fiber optic component plant in Kanata, Ontario.

CASE STUDY
MITEL

Mitel is a high-tech company with its headquarters in Kanata, Ontario, part of Silicon Valley North. It produces integrated circuits and silicon chips for computers. It also manufactures medical equipment, such as pacemakers, and develops voice communication systems. It is a transnational company that now operates in more than 100 countries, including the United States, the United Kingdom, China and Singapore, and employs 6,300 people worldwide.

TOURISM

Although Canada has huge and mainly empty tracts of wilderness, it has many other attractions for visitors, including large cosmopolitan cities. Tourists can immerse themselves in French-Canadian culture in cities such as Quebec or they can visit Vancouver's Chinatown for an Asian flavor.

Around 60 percent of all visitors travel to Ontario, and even within this one province they can see a huge variety of sights, from the cityscape of Toronto to Niagara Falls and the Great Lakes, and from Algonquin Provincial Park to the frozen shores of Hudson Bay.

NIAGARA FALLS

Niagara Falls are the most-visited attraction in Canada, with more than 14 million visitors each year. The falls consist of the American and Bridal Veil Falls on the US side and the broad Horseshoe Falls on the Canadian side. Visitors can stand right next to the top of the 50m-high Horseshoe Falls and watch millions of liters of water rush over the edge every second. Tourists can even get up close to the base of the waterfalls by taking a ride in one of the "Maid of the Mists" boats.

Tourists get covered in spray as they view the spectacular Niagara Falls.

COUNTRIES OF ORIGIN FOR CANADA'S VISITORS, 2003

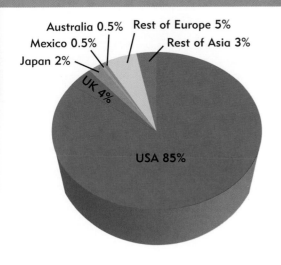

Australia 0.5% Rest of Europe 5%
Mexico 0.5% Rest of Asia 3%
Japan 2%
UK 4%
USA 85%

Source: Statistics Canada

IN THE WILD

Wilderness travel is increasing in popularity. Tourists can enjoy canoe trips on rivers such as the Mackenzie, usually with an Inuit guide. There are national parks, such as at Banff, where visitors can take part in a range of outdoor pursuits or simply enjoy the stunning views of glaciers, mountains and lakes. Hiking is particularly popular in summer and there are many marked trails. There is also good-quality skiing in winter.

Churchill, in northern Manitoba, is known as the "Polar Bear Capital of the World." Visitors can view polar bears from the relative safety of tundra buggies, specially adapted buses

that ride on giant tractor wheels. In a tundra buggy, people can get very close to the bears to take photographs while staying beyond the reach of their powerful paws.

The government and people of Canada are very aware of green issues and are trying to develop and expand their tourist industry

Tundra buggies like this one enable tourists to get a safe, close-up view of polar bears in Churchill, Manitoba.

while avoiding excessive development that would damage the very sights that visitors come to see.

CASE STUDY
KIMBERLEY, BRITISH COLUMBIA

Kimberley is Canada's highest town (1,113m above sea level) and for years it was the center of an important lead- and zinc-mining region. By the 1970s, most of the mines were closed and the townspeople were worried about finding work in the future. They took the unusual step of recreating Kimberley as a Bavarian (southern German) town in order to develop a tourist industry. Houses were given fake Bavarian-style fronts with wooden balconies; the world's largest cuckoo clock was installed in the town; and Bavarian food, drink and music replaced the fast food outlets and pop music. Eleven kilometers of the old mining railway have been restored to offer visitors a scenic ride through the region.

The idea seems to have worked and the town has increasing numbers of tourists, including many Germans. It looks as if Kimberley has a secure future.

Happy Hans is the Bavarian-style mascot of Kimberley, British Columbia.

TRANSPORT, ENERGY AND THE ENVIRONMENT

A passenger train in Alberta. Many long-distance trains have viewing platforms and observation cars to take full advantage of the passing scenery.

TRANSPORT

Despite its enormous size, Canada has a well-developed and modern transportation system. However, until railways were built in the late nineteenth century, long-distance travel was done mainly by water. Both the First Nations and early European settlers used rivers to move about the country. With the coming of the railway, the western part of Canada opened up to new settlement and European settlers began to spread beyond the eastern provinces of Ontario and Quebec.

RAIL

In 1885, the east of the country was linked to the Pacific coast at Vancouver by the Canadian Pacific Railway, which is still an important rail freight carrier across the country. This was when the Prairie provinces really developed. Wheat was transported east by rail to Thunder Bay on Lake Superior, where it was loaded onto ships for export. Branches off the main railway go north to access other resources. Rail is still the most economical way of moving containerized products or bulk goods such as coal, and today's trains mainly carry goods rather than people.

AIR

Air travel is important in Canada for a number of reasons – for international journeys, for accessing isolated settlements that may not have road links, and for traveling the often vast distances between different parts of the country. Canada has 13 international airports, including Toronto, Montreal, Vancouver and Halifax, and more than 300 smaller ones. Air Canada's fleet of 336 aircraft links 21 Canadian cities, 30 destinations in the United States and 56 other countries around the world.

TRANSPORT

Legend:
— Main road
···· Railway
✈ International airport

ARCTIC OCEAN

N

ALASKA (USA)

Whitehorse
Yellowknife
Iqaluit
Churchill
Hudson Bay
Prince Rupert
Edmonton
St John's
Vancouver
Calgary
Regina
Winnipeg
Quebec
Halifax
Montreal
Ottawa
PACIFIC OCEAN
Toronto
ATLANTIC OCEAN

0   1500 km
0   1000 miles

ROADS

Canada has more than 900,000km of highways and roads, and 60 percent of trade with the United States goes by road. North of Canada's transcontinental railway line, roads are more important than rail for carrying goods. By 2001 there were about 600 vehicles for every 1,000 people in Canada.

Recent developments have included building the world's longest bridge over ice-covered water. The Confederation Bridge is a permanent 13km link between Prince Edward Island and New Brunswick. Opened in 1997, it is part of the Trans-Canada Highway system. Another development is the opening of Highway 407, which is the first all-electronic toll road. It was built in northern Toronto to help alleviate traffic congestion on one of the busiest routes in Canada. It uses automatic vehicle recognition, and users' accounts are debited with the correct amount for the distance traveled. Future plans include weight-monitoring systems set within the road surface to check that trucks carrying goods are not overloaded and potentially dangerous.

SHIPPING

The eastern seaports, such as Halifax and Montreal, are important for exporting Canadian goods and receiving European imports to both Canada and the United States. However, Vancouver, on the west coast, has become Canada's busiest port, because much shipping trade is now focused on the Pacific Rim countries. Shipping traffic is also very important within and through the Great Lakes and the St Lawrence Seaway. The number of cruise ships calling at Canadian ports has increased recently, and in 2000 more than a million cruise ship passengers arrived.

CITY TRAVEL

Several cities, including Toronto, have underground railway systems or subways, and these are integrated with bus and tram timetables so that they all link up. Toronto also has a Light Rapid Transit Line that operates from the city center to the harborfront area. The Canadian government continues to encourage use of public transport, especially within urban areas, not only to reduce fossil fuel consumption but also to improve air quality for residents.

A cargo ship entering a lock on the St Lawrence Seaway.

ELECTRICITY SUPPLY BY SOURCE, 2001 (% OF TOTAL)

HEP	60
Fossil Fuels	26
Nuclear	13
Alternative	1

Source: Natural Resources Canada

ENERGY

Canada is rich in energy resources, especially HEP and fossil fuels. The energy sector is important to the Canadian economy, providing 6.8 percent of GDP and employing more than 280,000 people. Much of the energy produced is exported, 91 percent of it to the United States. Energy resources are not spread evenly: Most are in the west and north of the country, whereas the greatest demand and most electricity generation are in the east.

The separating plant and refinery for oil sands in Alberta.

HEP

Canada has many fast-flowing rivers and has harnessed this energy by building HEP plants on rivers such as the Fraser River in British Columbia and La Grande River on James Bay in Quebec.

FOSSIL FUELS

Canada's large oil and gas deposits, in Alberta and the far north, are extracted and transported by pipeline to the east of the country, where the demand is heaviest. The newer oil and gas rigs that are now situated off the coast of Newfoundland have been built to withstand the impact of the icebergs that regularly travel along this part of the coast. Most of Canada's coal is exported, though 87 percent of the rest is used for electricity generation.

ENERGY SUPPLY BY SOURCE, 2003 (% OF TOTAL)

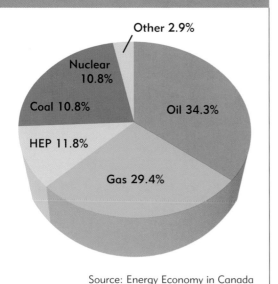

Other 2.9%
Nuclear 10.8%
Coal 10.8%
Oil 34.3%
HEP 11.8%
Gas 29.4%

Source: Energy Economy in Canada

ENERGY USE BY SECTOR, 2001 (% OF TOTAL)

Residential	17
Commercial	13
Industrial	39
Transportation	29
Agriculture	2

Source: Natural Resources Canada

A row of wind generators in southern Alberta.

NUCLEAR POWER

Most of Canada's 22 nuclear power stations are in Ontario. Because of safety problems, several older stations have been shut down well before their expected 40-year lifespan expired. Many reactors urgently need upgrading, but at present this is not a popular option with the Canadian public. Nuclear power production has fallen by a third since 1994, and this decline is likely to continue.

ALTERNATIVE ENERGY SOURCES

Apart from HEP, alternative energy sources provide only 1 percent of Canada's electricity at present. This is set to increase because there is much government and public support for more environmentally friendly forms of power generation. Tidal power is being used in the Bay of Fundy, in Nova Scotia, which has a tidal range of 17m, the largest in the world. As yet there is only one large tidal power station but it produces enough electricity each year for 4,000 homes. Several sites along the coast north of Vancouver have been identified as being suitable for the development of wave power. Wind power is in its early stages of development in Canada, and there is a growth of interest in photovoltaic cells to produce solar power.

CASE STUDY
JAMES BAY HEP SYSTEM

The huge dam spillway at James Bay. Nearby is the world's largest underground powerhouse.

A third of Canada's rivers flow into James Bay, at the southern end of Hudson Bay. In 1972 a HEP project built dams on La Grande River and diverted four other rivers into La Grande to provide more energy. This first phase was completed by 1985, leaving 11,341km² of forest flooded as reservoirs covered the land behind the dams. This development had serious consequences for the environment. Rivers important for wildlife suffered from reduced flow as their waters were diverted into the scheme. Stagnant water covered the flooded forest and released methane, a greenhouse gas, in huge quantities. Another impact was on the lives of the First Nations people who lived in the area and who had not been consulted about the project. By the time Phase 2 was begun in 1989, Canadians were much more aware of environmental issues, and the First Nations were involved in the decision-making process. During this phase, the world's largest dam and underground generating station, La Grande Two, was built. The planned development is still incomplete as there is much opposition to the latest phase.

WILD CANADA

Although much of Canada is sparsely populated, there is still a need to protect the wild animals and natural landscapes from threats. Companies that want to explore wilderness areas to find and extract fossil fuels, such as oil, pose some of these threats.

There is also pressure from those involved in the tourism industry to allow the further development of hotels and facilities in scenic areas. To help protect its wild areas, Canada has 39 national parks and three marine reserves. There are also more than 1,000 provincial parks, which are run by the provincial governments.

CASE STUDY
BANFF NATIONAL PARK

A spectacular view of ice fields and mountains in Banff National Park.

Banff is the oldest Canadian national park, and it borders three others – Jasper, Yoho and Kootenay, and three local provincial parks. The combined area of these parks is called the Canadian Rocky Mountain Parks World Heritage Site.

Despite this, there are still wildlife species under severe threat from human use of the parks. Much development has taken place in and around the town of Banff, because it has some flat land, which is in short supply. Formerly timber wolves used this flat land as they moved from one hunting ground to another, but the wolves cannot cope with the presence of so many humans and their numbers have plummeted. The warm-water springs near Banff are home to a small species of snail, the Banff Springs snail, which is found nowhere else in the world. It has been brought back from the edge of extinction but there are still only about 3,000 living in just five pools. People are banned from swimming in the pools because the chemicals contained in their deodorant, insect repellent and other such products are toxic to the snails and can kill them. Despite this, each year some people disobey the rules and cause serious damage to the snail population. If the snails cannot survive in such a heavily protected area, what hope is there for other species?

Every year, 4 million visitors go to enjoy Banff's mountain scenery interspersed with glaciers and rivers. There is much wildlife to see, and visitors get very excited when they spot a black bear or grizzly bear. The traffic usually comes to a standstill, known as a "bear jam," as everyone tries to get a look. The problem the park managers have is that the huge numbers of visitors are damaging the very landscape they have come to see. They do this by eroding footpaths, polluting the air with their cars, and scaring the animals away from their usual hunting and breeding grounds. Building facilities for visitors, such as toilets and stores, reduces the amount of untouched land for wildlife.

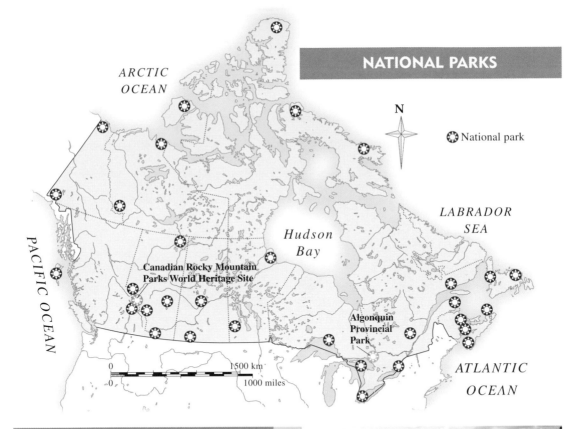

NATIONAL PARKS

ARCTIC
OCEAN

N

✸ National park

PACIFIC OCEAN

*Hudson
Bay*

*LABRADOR
SEA*

**Canadian Rocky Mountain
Parks World Heritage Site**

**Algonquin
Provincial
Park**

*ATLANTIC
OCEAN*

```
0                    1500 km
|_____|
0                    1000 miles
```

The oldest and largest of Ontario's
provincial parks, Algonquin Provincial Park
was set up in 1893 to provide an area for
outdoor recreation, to protect forest areas
and to allow some mineral extraction to
support the local economy. Park managers
have divided the area into zones giving
different levels of access and protection.
Located just a few hours away from large
centers of population, such as Toronto and
Ottawa, the park provides an ideal
weekend escape to a wilder landscape.

Canoeing in the Algonquin Provincial Park.

ZONES OF ALGONQUIN PROVINCIAL PARK

Nature reserve, wilderness and natural environment	18.8%
Development and access	3.1%
Recreation	77.9%
Historical	0.1%

53

CANADA AND THE WORLD

Queen Elizabeth II meets First Nation representatives at The Forks in Winnipeg, Manitoba, in 2002.

Canada is known for its tolerance and enjoys good relationships, both economic and political, with most countries of the world. Its large reserves of natural resources form a basis for much of its exports, such as wood pulp (for use in paper manufacture), timber, aluminum, chemicals and oil. However, it also exports industrial machinery and a wide range of telecommunications equipment.

MAJOR TRADING PARTNERS (% OF VALUE), 2003

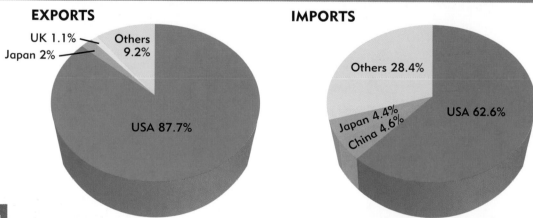

EXPORTS

UK 1.1%
Japan 2%
Others 9.2%
USA 87.7%

IMPORTS

Others 28.4%
Japan 4.4%
China 4.6%
USA 62.6%

Source: *CIA World Factbook, 2004*

The North American Free Trade Agreement (NAFTA)

Canada's main trading partner is the United States, but it also has strong trading links with Mexico. In 1994 the three countries created a trading bloc called the North American Free Trade Agreement (NAFTA). Its aim is to remove tariffs (trade taxes) and other barriers to free trade in order to better compete with other large trading groups such as the European Union (EU). NAFTA differs from other trading blocs in that Mexico is a developing country linked to two developed manufacturing giants. Unlike the EU agreements, NAFTA only covers trade and does not allow the free movement of labor between member countries. Canada's exports to both the United States and Mexico have increased as a result of the agreement.

Asia-Pacific Economic Cooperation (APEC)

Canada's Pacific coastline grew in importance during the later years of the twentieth century, as new markets opened up in the Pacific Rim countries. These countries, located around the edges of the Pacific Ocean, include newly industrialized nations, such as South Korea, China and Malaysia, as well as more established industrialized areas, such as Australia and Singapore. APEC was set up in 1989 to encourage greater cooperation and trade between its members, and the port of Vancouver has benefited from the growth in trade.

The Commonwealth

Canada is an important member of the Commonwealth, a voluntary association of 54 independent states that once had colonial links with the United Kingdom. A main principle of the Commonwealth is the pursuit of international peace, and this fits in well with Canada's UN membership and its own aims within international relationships.

Other Organizations

Canada is a member of many other international organizations including the North Atlantic Treaty Organization (NATO). Within NATO it provides peacekeeping troops for Afghanistan and also for the Stabilization Force (SFOR) in Bosnia-Herzegovina.

Canada is a member of the Group of Eight (G8), which is made up of major democratic countries that meet to deal with important economic and political issues. The other members are the United States, the United Kingdom, Japan, Germany, France, Italy and Russia. Recent G8 meetings have addressed illegal logging and global health problems, such as AIDS.

Canada is also one of the 191 members of the United Nations (UN) and was a founding member of another section of the UN, the United Nations Educational, Scientific and Cultural Organization (UNESCO), in 1946. Throughout the history of the UN, Canada has made significant contributions to all areas, including peacekeeping, providing aid for development, promoting human rights and reducing environmental problems. It is the seventh-largest contributor of funds to the UN. In 2003 this amounted to Can$53.4 million plus a further Can$77 million toward peacekeeping costs. There is a great deal of support for the UN among Canadian citizens and there are United Nations Associations in many cities across the country. They arrange discussions and exhibitions and develop links in schools and universities.

Prime Minister Paul Martin of Canada shakes hands with Prime Minister Junichiro Koizumi of Japan at a G8 Summit.

CANADA'S ECOLOGICAL FOOTPRINT

It takes resources to support people. One way to measure how much of Earth's resources it takes to support a country's lifestyle is to calculate its ecological footprint (see fact box below). This measurement includes demand for water, energy, food and resources as well as the disposal of any wastes. It is usually given as the number of hectares of land needed per person. At 7.7 hectares, Canada's ecological footprint is the third largest in the world, after the United States and Australia.

The Athabasca Glacier is part of the Columbia Icefield in Alberta. The glacier is melting at 10–15m per year due to global warming.

Although Canada is rich in natural resources, since the 1980s Canadians have become more aware of the impact of resource extraction on the environment. They have also become alert to wider issues, such as global warming, the impact of acid rain, and the need for sustainable development. Replanting of logged areas is now commonplace, as is the restoration of landscapes after mining has finished in an area. Quotas (fixed numbers that are set after research) are used to limit the number of fish that can be caught in rivers or the numbers of an animal, such as the elk, that can be hunted in any one year.

GREEN MOVEMENTS

There are many active conservation and green organizations in Canada. Some are branches of global organizations, such as Greenpeace and Friends of the Earth. At least one, the Sierra Club of Canada, is a branch of an influential US movement, but there are also many Canadian organizations such as the Canadian Nature Federation (CNF). Like many of the Canadian people themselves, these groups are concerned about a wide range of local, national and global issues, such as the damage caused by resource extraction (including pollution and habitat loss), the effects of industrial and vehicle emissions on acid rain and global warming, and the need to promote sustainability. The CNF's aims are specific to Canada: to protect and conserve the country's natural diversity and promote a better understanding of nature through education.

ECOLOGICAL FOOTPRINTS OF SELECTED COUNTRIES

COUNTRY	FOOTPRINT IN HECTARES
USA	10.3
Australia	9.0
Canada	7.7
UK	5.2
Mexico	2.6
China	1.2
Pakistan	0.8

Source: Earth Council, Canada

An anti-logging protest on a road on Vancouver Island, British Columbia.

DISAPPEARANCES

Over the last 150 years, 12 Canadian species have become extinct, including the woodland caribou and the Labrador duck. A further 380 species are on the "at risk register" of Canada, including the last remaining 37 Vancouver Island marmots, which are likely to become extinct by 2025. Global warming is also changing habitat conditions, as the Arctic ice melts earlier and freezes later, and this is causing problems for some species. For example, seals need ice floes on which to give birth to their pups in the spring. If the ice melts too soon, the seals have to give birth on land where they are far more vulnerable to predators.

THE FUTURE

Canadians have one of the highest standards of living in the world and yet have a genuine and deep-seated love of wilderness and the outdoors. Through education and the work of the many green movements they are becoming more aware of the impacts of their lifestyle on their surroundings. For example, 90 percent of Canadians are worried about the state of the environment. Most Canadians recycle, and there is an understanding of the need to reduce dependence on fossil fuels. Pressure from the green movements and from Canadians themselves is gradually encouraging industry and the government to think more sustainably, so that Canada can continue to provide both economic resources and undamaged landscapes for future generations.

Sustainable forestry: Trees are planted at Kispiox Valley, British Columbia, to replace those felled.

GLOSSARY

Acid rain Rain containing sulfur and nitrogen oxides that have come from emissions from factories, power stations and vehicles.

Agribusiness Commercial farming that is on an industrial scale and is highly mechanized, often run as partnerships between a finance company and an agricultural management firm.

Agrotourism Tourism that is farm based and includes farm tours, farm stays and creation of nature reserves for public access.

Birth rate The number of live births per 1,000 population in a year.

BSE (bovine spongiform encephalopathy) A disease that affects the brains of cattle and can be passed to humans via the food chain.

CBD (central business district) The area of town or city where most of the commercial activity is found.

Coniferous Trees that are cone bearing and usually evergreen (they keep their leaves year-round).

Death rate The number of deaths per 1,000 population in a year.

Deciduous Describes broad-leaved trees, such as oak and maple, that lose their leaves in autumn.

Delta An area of land at the mouth of a river where sediment has been deposited, often in a triangular shape.

Drainage basin The area of land drained by a river and its tributaries.

E-commerce The practice of using the World Wide Web in order to carry out business.

Emissions Waste gases given off to the atmosphere by factory chimneys and the exhausts of vehicles.

First Nation peoples The term used in Canada for the earliest settlers of North America, who came across from Asia; Native Americans.

Fold mountains Relatively young mountains formed through folding of the layers of rocks under pressure. Many of these mountains are still increasing in height.

GDP (Gross Domestic Product) The total value of a country's goods. Often quoted as per capita, that is, the amount per person.

GNI (Gross National Income) The total value of everything produced by industry and services within a country and earned by that country abroad.

HEP (hydroelectric power) Electricity generated by water as it passes through turbines.

High-tech industries Industries that use the most up-to-date technology, such as aerospace and computing.

Ice age A period in the Earth's history in which large areas of land are covered by ice sheets and glaciers and undergo both erosion and deposition.

Intensive agriculture A farming system in which there is a high level of inputs, such as labor and chemicals, per hectare.

Inuit Meaning "The People," this is the preferred name for tribes formerly known as Eskimo.

Mechanization The process by which work previously done by humans or animals is taken over by machines.

Muskeg A boggy landscape of northern Canada that consists of sphagnum moss blanket bog and very few trees.

Overfishing Catching more fish than can be replaced naturally.

Permafrost A layer of permanently frozen soil, found near the surface in Arctic regions of Canada.

Plain A large area of flat land.

Prairie A large, generally flat, grassland area with very few trees.

Rain shadow An area on the leeward side of a mountain range that receives relatively little rainfall because most has already fallen on the windward side.

Sedimentary rock Rock formed from deposits created by wind, ice or water and then forced together under pressure. Example are sandstone and limestone.

Subduction The process of one tectonic plate descending beneath another.

Sustainable development The development of resources that meets the needs of the present population without compromising the ability of future generations to meet their needs.

Tectonic plate One of the large crustal plates that make up the Earth's surface.

Temperate rain forest A type of forest found in areas of warm summers and cool winters with heavy rainfall all year. It has less diversity than a tropical rain forest.

Tornado A violent revolving storm that is formed over rapidly heated land.

Transnational company A company that operates in several countries.

Tree line The location beyond which trees can no longer survive. This can be in the north of Canada or partway up a mountain.

Tributary A river that joins a larger river.

Tundra A high-latitude region where it is too cold for trees to grow. Tundra vegetation is dominated by mosses and lichens.

FURTHER INFORMATION

BOOKS TO READ:

Eyewitness Travel Guides: Canada. Rev. ed. New York: Dorling Kindersley, 2003. A good general guide to all parts of Canada, highly illustrated.

Montgomery, L. M. *Anne of Green Gables.* New York: Bantam Books, 1998. The classic fictional tale of Anne, an orphan, sent to live in a small community on Prince Edward Island in the early 1900s.

Riendeau, Roger. *A Brief History of Canada.* New York: Facts On File, 1999. A wealth of information on Canadian history.

Roste, Vaughn. *The Xenophobe's Guide to the Canadians.* London: Oval Books, 2002. A humorous guide to the customs and ways of Canadians.

WEBSITES:

GENERAL INFORMATION:
Government of Canada: About Canada
http://canada.gc.ca/acanada/acPubHome.jsp?lang-eng
A range of Internet links about the country.

ENVIRONMENT:
Canadian Nature Federation
http://www.cnf.ca/
Information on wildlife, the environment and emerging issues.

NATIONAL PARKS:
Parks Canada
www.parkscanada.ca/
Information and articles about Canada's many national parks.

NUNAVUT:
The Government of Nunavut
http://www.gov.nu.ca/
Fact sheets available for download on aspects of life in this newly created Canadian territory.

QUEBEC:
Explore Quebec
http://www.bonjourquebec.com/anglais/explorez
Information and photos about this French-speaking province. As with many Canadian websites, you can also access this site in French.

METRIC CONVERSION TABLE

To convert	to	do this
mm (millimeters)	inches	divide by 25.4
cm (centimeters)	inches	divide by 2.54
m (meters)	feet	multiply by 3.281
m (meters)	yards	multiply by 1.094
km (kilometers)	yards	multiply by 1094
km (kilometers)	miles	divide by 1.6093
kilometers per hour	miles per hour	divide by 1.6093
cm^2 (square centimeters)	square inches	divide by 6.452
m^2 (square meters)	square feet	multiply by 10.76
m^2 (square meters)	square yards	multiply by 1.196
km^2 (square kilometers)	square miles	divide by 2.59
km^2 (square kilometers)	acres	multiply by 247.1
hectares	acres	multiply by 2.471
cm^3 (cubic centimeters)	cubic inches	multiply by 16.387
m^3 (cubic meters)	cubic yards	multiply by 1.308
l (liters)	pints	multiply by 2.113
l (liters)	gallons	divide by 3.785
g (grams)	ounces	divide by 28.329
kg (kilograms)	pounds	multiply by 2.205
metric tonnes	short tons	multiply by 1.1023
metric tonnes	long tons	multiply by 0.9842
BTUs (British thermal units)	kWh (kilowatt-hours)	divide by 3,415.3
watts	horsepower	multiply by 0.001341
kWh (kilowatt-hours)	horsepower-hours	multiply by 1.341
MW (megawatts)	horsepower	multiply by 1,341
gigawatts per hour	horsepower per hour	multiply by 1,341,000
°C (degrees Celsius)	°F (degrees Fahrenheit)	multiply by 1.8 then add 32

INDEX

Numbers shown in **bold** refer to pages with maps, graphic illustrations or photographs.

A First Nation totem pole at Stanley Park, in Vancouver, British Columbia.

Snowmobiling in Canada's
frozen north.